by Garry Chapman

SURF

WARNING:

Extreme sports can be very dangerous. Mishaps can result in death or serious injury.
Seek expert advice before attempting any of the stunts you read about in this book.

This book is for my daughter Casey.

This edition first published in 2002 in the United States of America by Chelsea House Publishers, a subsidiary of Haights Cross Communications.

Chelsea House Publishers
1974 Sproul Road, Suite 400
Broomall, PA 19008-0914

The Chelsea House world wide web address is www.chelseahouse.com

Library of Congress Cataloging-in-Publication Data Applied for.

ISBN 0-7910-6611-8

First published in 2001 by
Macmillan Education Australia Pty Ltd
627 Chapel Street, South Yarra, Australia, 3141

Copyright © Garry Chapman 2001

Edited by Renée Otmar, Otmar Miller Consultancy Pty Ltd
Text design by if design
Cover design by if design
Printed in China

Acknowledgements
The author and the publisher are grateful to the following for permission to reproduce copyright material:

Cover photo of boardsurfer courtesy of Sport. The Library/Tony Harrington.

Allsport, pp. 6, 10–11, 13; Australian Picture Library/Corbis, pp. 14, 15; Coo-ee Historical Picture Library, p. 4; Photolibrary.com/Bruce Forster, p. 5; Sport. The Library/Col Stewart, p. 24 (insert); Sport. The Library/Jason Childs, pp. 7–9, 12, 16–19, 21; Sport. The Library/John Carter, pp. 22–23, 24–25; Sport. The Library/Rudiger Fessel, pp. 22, 30; Sport. The Library/Stefan Hunziker, pp. 27, 28; Sport. The Library/Tony Harrington, p. 20; Sporting Images/Duane Hart, pp. 26, 29.

While every care has been taken to trace and acknowledge copyright the publishers tender their apologies for any accidental infringement where copyright has proved untraceable.

DISCLAIMER
The extreme sports described in this book are potentially dangerous, and can result in death or serious injury if attempted by inexperienced persons. The author and the publishers wish to advise readers that they take no responsibility for any mishaps that may occur as the result of persons attempting to perform the activities described in this book.

Contents

THE SEA SCENE

A fascination for the sea

People have held a fascination for the sea for thousands of years. Ancient cultures believed that great gods and fearsome monsters inhabited the sea. Family elders passed on to the next generation stories about the sea. Many people chose to live within easy reach of the sea.

The sea's rewards

For some, the sea held generous rewards. Traders discovered sea routes that took them to strange and exotic places. The sea provided a way to transport goods from other countries, such as delicate silks and fragrant spices. Brave explorers sailed across uncharted oceans in search of wealth and new colonies. The fisherfolk of coastal villages put out to sea each morning in small boats and returned home each evening, their boats brimming with the day's catch.

Fear of the sea

Other people feared the sea. They watched as great storms formed out over the ocean then gathered strength and swept in across the coast, destroying entire villages and leaving death and misery. Fishing boats and merchant ships left ports and were never heard from again. Superstitious sailors refused to leave the safety of port if they sensed the sea was in an angry mood. It was generally unheard of to set foot in the sea unless you had a very good reason for doing so.

The first surfers

More than 200 years ago, while on the Hawaiian islands, Captain James Cook and his crew watched with amazement as the islanders rode the waves and played in the surf. To this day, Hawaii remains the heart and soul of surfing culture.

Bathing in an earlier era

Stories filtered back to Europe about the Hawaiians' strange antics, but few others were bold enough to venture into the surf for their recreation. Some Europeans took to visiting bathing beaches. Bathers wore costumes that covered them from ankle to neck. Men and women bathed at separate beaches. Very few bathers ventured out beyond waist depth, because they could not swim.

Hawaii has always been considered the home of surfing.

TAKING SURFING TO EXTREMES

GLOSSARY

jet skis – small, motor-driven watercraft used for towing surfers into big waves and for performing fast rescues

This statue of Duke Kahanamoku was erected at Waikiki Beach in Hawaii to honor the legendary surfer.

Xtreme Fact

Thomas Edison captured the first film footage of surfing at Waikiki Beach in 1898. One hundred years later, on 'Big Wednesday', IMAX cameras captured big wave surfers on Oahu's North Shore for the movie *Extreme*.

Duke brings surfing to the world

Over time, people began to find new ways to enjoy the beach. More and more people learned to swim. The fame of surfing spread as Hawaiian Duke Kahanamoku toured the world, demonstrating his prowess with a massive surfboard. Thousands turned out to see him wherever he went, and many kept surfing when he moved on.

Surf culture

In Hawaii, the surf culture remained strong. Along the Pacific Ocean coasts of Australia and California, the popularity of surfing grew and grew. Hundreds of thousands of people visited these beaches annually. Many boldly ventured out into the breakers to surf, swim and play. Surf lifesaving clubs sprang up at all major beaches.

New ways to enjoy the surf

Recent technological developments have brought about exciting variations on traditional surfing. Surfers are towed behind **jet skis** to ride monster ocean waves. Bodyboarders have discovered ways to push the limits on a board, without having to stand up. Boardsailors attach sails to boards in order to perform awesome aerial tricks with wind and waves. Wakeboarders seek calmer waters in which to perform their magic. People still have good reason to fear the sea, but they now also know how to have fun in the surf.

Surfing Hot Spots

Hawaii

Every day, the most revered surf in the world pounds the ocean beaches of the Hawaiian Islands. Massive **swells** start to build in the icy waters off the Aleutian Islands, thousands of miles to the north. They travel for two days in an uninterrupted southerly direction across the Pacific Ocean, to reach Hawaii.

MASSIVE WAVES

The swells are barely visible as they race over the deep ocean bed, but when they come up against the steep reef that lies just offshore of Hawaii, they are instantly squeezed inward and upward. The swells, previously moving at speeds of up to 80 kilometers (50 miles) per hour, slow down considerably. This causes the water to pile up until it forms massive peaks, several feet high, which then crash forward over themselves as breaking waves.

FABLED BEACHES

Many of the world's top surfers, bodyboarders and boardsailors make Hawaii their home. This means they are only minutes away when the really monstrous surf comes in, as it does up to ten times a year. Many of Hawaii's fabled beaches are located on the island of Oahu, and include Waikiki Beach, Waimea Bay and the North Shore.

JAWS

Perhaps the most awesome wave in the world is Jaws, a perfectly shaped giant with a deep blue face. Jaws consistently rises to between 12 and 18 meters (40 to 60 feet) in height. A barrel is formed as the lip curls over and begins to collapse. Jaws crashes down with explosive force and a deafening roar, sending tons of water racing towards the volcanic rocks. Since waves travel in **sets**, a number of these colossal giants arrive in close succession.

California

Great surf beaches can be found elsewhere in the Pacific Ocean. The surf coast of California in the United States stretches more than 2,500 kilometers (1,554 miles). It is dotted with legendary surf beaches such as La Jolla, Malibu and Ventura. A recently discovered surfing mecca is the spot called Maverick's, near San Francisco. Maverick's consistently produces bigger waves than anywhere else along the coast.

Australia

Australia also receives more than its fair share of great surf from the Pacific Ocean. Many surfers make the road trip north from places such as Torquay and Bells Beach on the Victorian Surf Coast. Along the way they might stop to sample the waves at beaches such as Ulladulla, Cronulla and Newcastle in New South Wales, before arriving at the sunny Queensland beaches of Kirra and Noosa.

Tahiti and Fiji

The Pacific islands of Tahiti and Fiji are world-class surf destinations which receive big swells that originate from the waters around Antarctica. Fiji and Tahiti are composed of many small islands surrounded by coral reefs. The best waves can be found in the breaks between the coral reefs.

Bali

Bali, a small island in the Indonesian chain of islands, is a very popular surf destination. Thousands of surfers, bodyboarders and boardsailors arrive each year to spend their annual holidays among the waves of Kuta and Legian beaches.

Brazil

Some of the best Atlantic Ocean surf can be found on the beautiful sandy beaches of Brazil, in South America. The country has a very long coastline and many fine surf beaches. Some of the most popular beaches are concentrated around the big cities of Rio de Janeiro and São Paolo.

South Africa

The Agulhas Current of the Indian Ocean brings warm water all year-round to the east coast of South Africa. Large crowds of surfers are regularly drawn to the string of excellent surf beaches located along the coast surrounding the city of Durban.

Xtreme Fact

In April 1868, a tsunami slammed the coast of Hawaii. It is said that, in order to save his own life, a Hawaiian named Holua surfed what was then the biggest wave in history, a monster approaching 15 meters (50 feet) in height.

The surf in Hawaii is certainly the most revered in the world. Here spectators watch the 1994 international Pipeline Masters competition.

Gear Up for the Surf

PROTECT THE SKIN

Traditionally, surfers never required much more than a pair of board shorts to enjoy the waves. Their bronzed torsos were exposed constantly to the sun's bright rays. People are now more aware that too much sun can seriously damage the skin. It may even cause deadly skin cancer. Today, surf clothing manufacturers lead the way in developing gear that protects the skin from harmful radiation.

Most surfers cover up sensibly before taking to the waves. They wear a combination of surf vest and board shorts, which offer sun protection and provide the freedom of movement that surfers, bodyboarders and boardsailors require. A liberal application of sunscreen protects the exposed skin.

AVOID HYPOTHERMIA

Surfers in colder waters also require protection from the cold. Often, the waves start from ocean swells that have travelled from much colder regions of the Earth. There is always a danger that exposure to cold water for too long can bring about **hypothermia**.

Wear a wetsuit

The best protection from the cold when surfing is to wear a **neoprene** wetsuit. Wetsuits are made in a variety of thicknesses, depending on the degree of warmth required. Some wetsuits provide enough warmth that surfers can enjoy their sport in the middle of winter, when the surf is often at its wildest.

Even in summertime, a neoprene wetsuit provides the best protection for the skin. Australian surfing legend Mark Occhilupo, 1999.

HOLD ONTO THE BOARD

Surfers and bodyboarders often wear wrist straps or leg ropes to attach themselves to their boards. The leash ensures that, whenever a surfer **wipes out**, the board can be retrieved easily. Otherwise, they may have to waste valuable time searching for their board, which the breaking surf may have carried in most of the way to the beach.

PROTECT THE EYES

An important item for those exposed to the sun glinting off the water all day is a pair of good quality sunglasses. They provide protection from the sun's ultraviolet rays, which can be quite harmful to the eyes.

TAKE PRIDE IN THE SPORT

The surfing community prides itself on the very popular range of surf clothing. Surf clothing is a favorite of young people all around the world, including those who have never ridden a wave in their lives. Surf clothing includes Hawaiian-style print shirts, windbreakers, T-shirts, board shorts, sandals and headgear.

Many items of surf clothing prominently feature the brand name of the manufacturer. The makers of surf clothing sponsor big tournaments and some of the world's top professional board riders. Many of these clothing manufacturers also make boards and related paraphernalia.

Xtreme Fact

Modern wetsuits have a number of hi-tech design features. These include watertight seals at the neck and wrists, contoured kneepads and lumbar support for the lower back.

Safety in the Surf

Minimize the risks

It is a sad fact that heavy surf has taken many lives over the years. Surfers who wipe out on the face of a monstrous wave may find themselves struggling to resurface as tons of water come tumbling down on top of them. Every second is crucial as they fight with every ounce of strength to reach the life-giving oxygen above. Waves come in sets, and if they do not make the surface within about 20 seconds, the next wave will soon arrive. Some of the world's top professional surfers have died because they just could not reach the surface in time. One way surfers minimize the risk of being held under by coming waves is to let the first few waves of a set pass before they catch one.

Stay in peak condition

Keep yourself in peak physical condition. In order to recover from a wipeout, you will need strength and the ability to hold your breath for an extended period. Prepare yourself for such an event by taking in deep breaths and filling your lungs with oxygen moments before you catch a wave.

Know your limits

Sometimes, surfing accidents occur because people over-estimate their ability to ride the big waves. Surf sports always look exciting, especially when the waves are awesome, but these conditions suit only those capable of handling them. If there is any doubt about a particular swell, it is much wiser to turn back and live to surf another day.

Wipeout! In order to recover from a wipeout you will need strength and the ability to hold your breath for an extended period.

Xtreme Fact

Surfing clinics are now conducted on many popular surf beaches every summer. People attend camps where they learn surfing skills and safety drills from some of the world's top surfers.

Never surf alone

Surf in the company of a buddy. You can keep an eye out for each other in the water. In the event of an accident, it is comforting to know that someone can be at your side within minutes, to keep you safe until rescuers arrive. If you or your surfing buddy needs help in a hurry, one of you can use the International Distress Code to alert others. In order to do this, sit on the board and keep raising both arms above your head and then lowering them to the sides of your body.

Obey the rules of surfing

Just as lives are saved on the roads by road safety rules, surfers also obey a set of rules intended to keep them safe. Some of these rules are:

- ☞ When two riders are paddling for the same wave, it belongs to the one closest to the breaking part of the wave.
- ☞ A rider should not drop in on another rider's wave.
- ☞ A surfer already riding a wave has right of way. Those paddling out must make every effort to stay out of the way.
- ☞ Treat other riders with respect.

Beware of jet skis

Tow-in surfing at big wave sites, such as at Waimea Bay and Maverick's, has resulted in an increase in the number of jet skis in the water. On days when the really big surf is up, these big breaks can become very crowded. In the interest of everyone's safety, be prepared to line up and wait your turn.

It is important to obey the rules of surfing when there are other surfers around.

Big wave surfing at Waimea Bay, Hawaii. It was here that Greg Noll created surfing history.

WAIMEA BAY'S GIANT WAVES

Waimea Bay is situated on the North Shore of the island of Oahu, in Hawaii. The waves that break there consistently reach heights of 12 meters (39 feet) or more. They result from huge ocean swells that race across the Pacific from far to the north. As they hit the outer reefs of Hawaii, the swells become awesome giant waves with almost vertical faces. Moments later, the waves collapse and explode.

GREG NOLL LIVES TO TELL THE TALE

Although many surfers had dreamed of riding the massive waves of Waimea Bay, none had been bold enough to attempt it. They simply assumed that waves of such magnitude were too big to be ridden. Greg Noll changed all that one day in 1957, when he paddled out and rode one of Waimea's huge breakers. He lived to tell the tale, and inspired a handful of others to tackle big wave surfing. Every November thereafter, a small group of brave surfers met to take on the first of the big winter swells as they arrived from the north.

NOLL RIDES A COLOSSUS

Twelve years later, Noll created history for a second time when he rode what was then the largest wave ever ridden. He paddled into a 10-meter (33 foot) **colossus**, successfully dropped onto its face, then looked up to see a mountain of water crashing down all over him. Noll jumped off his board seconds before the water hit, tumbling and tossing him over and over. He eventually emerged in one piece. Noll staggered onto the beach, briefly thought back over his career achievements, and quit surfing on the spot.

BIG WAVE SURFING

Courage, reflex and skill

Big wave surfing requires such courage, reflexes and skill, that to this day fewer than 100 people worldwide engage in this sport. The greater the challenge, the more respect riders earn within the surfing community. These surfers respect the power of nature. They understand that it will only take an instant of indecision for the sea to have the ultimate victory. They enjoy the **adrenaline rush** that a successful ride brings, yet safety remains uppermost in their thoughts.

Fitness and strength

Big wave surfing requires great physical fitness and strength.

Most riders spend weeks in training, preparing for the day the waves come in. They work hard to develop their breathing, which one day could be the difference between life and death. In order to achieve the paddle speed needed to drop into waves of this size, surfers need boards at least 3 meters (10 feet) in length.

The right wave

Out beyond the surf line, a surfer waits for a big set to come in. The first couple of waves are allowed to pass. The rider paddles hard as the sea beneath heaves up into an enormous peak. As the curl begins spilling over, the surfer stands and plunges down the wave's steep face. It is a thrilling moment.

The wave arches over and the rider accelerates across the smooth surface, dwarfed by the wall of water above. The wave crashes over itself, threatening to engulf board and rider, but the descent has been timed perfectly. The rider reaches the safety of a neighboring **trough** just a split second before the mountain of water makes its shattering impact.

Xtreme Fact

Big waves are not restricted to the Pacific Ocean. The first Big Wave Team World Championships were held in 2000 on the tiny island of Madeira in the North Atlantic Ocean, southwest of Portugal. Some of the wildest and biggest waves on the planet hosted the world's first big wave team event.

When surfing the big waves, timing is everything. You need to reach the safety of a neighboring trough before the mountain of water makes its shattering impact.

The power of Jaws

Hawaii's Jaws is an awesome wave. It rises about ten times each year, when conditions are just right. Jaws has been known to tower higher than 18 meters (59 feet) on occasions. The power of this wave lies beyond imagination. Its lip alone has enough force to snap your leg. The greater danger, however, is that you could be mercilessly trapped beneath this enormous volume of water until you drown.

COURAGEOUS BOARDSAILORS CONQUER JAWS

This huge element of risk, combined with the sheer power and beauty of the wave, is what attracts big wave surfers to Jaws. In the early 1980s, some courageous boardsailors successfully began riding the breathtaking **tubes** it formed. Within a short time, big wave surfers were also matching their skills against Jaws.

THEY STAY AHEAD OF THE CURL

After dropping onto the wave, the surfer must accelerate down the almost-vertical face of Jaws, always staying ahead of the rapidly breaking curl. The consequences could be dangerous if they fail to stay in front of this collapsing curl, or are unable to remain balanced on the board upon such a steep face.

JET SKI ASSISTANCE

Jaws is too big to paddle into. Boardsailors discovered that they had to be towed in on jet skis and propelled into the wave. Surfers adopted the same approach. There is no other way to get onto Jaws. When towing in a surfer, the jet ski heads down to the smooth channel beside the wave. As it reaches the trough at the bottom of the great wave, the jet ski darts in, snatches up the surfer, then retreats to a place of safety. This whole sequence must take no more than 20 seconds before the next wave crashes down.

Riding the Big Waves

Maverick's

Near Half Moon Bay, close to San Francisco, is Maverick's. Outside of Hawaii, it is the biggest surf break in the United States. After crossing 3,000 kilometers (1,864 feet) of open ocean, mountainous waves thunder into the headland. The water here is so cold that it saps energy and drastically reduces the time that surfers can hold their breath under water. Maverick's was first noticed in 1962, by a surfer who named the spot after his dog.

DANGEROUS ROCKS

When the surf is up at Maverick's, perfectly shaped, 12-meter (40 foot) breakers just keep on coming. They smash down dangerously close to jagged rocks. Some are exposed, but more lurk beneath the surface. When you surf at Maverick's, you take your life into your own hands. In contrast to Hawaii, it is possible to paddle onto the waves at Maverick's, but more and more riders are now towing-in using jet skis.

TRiUMPH AND TRAGEDY

Jeff Clark is known as the King of Maverick's. He first surfed it on a small board in the winter of 1974–75. Fifteen years later, Clark was still the only person to have surfed Maverick's. Today, Maverick's is surfed by a small but dedicated party of riders, but few ride it as well as Clark. One who managed to do so was 16-year-old Jay Moriarty, who on December 21, 1994 successfully rode a wave estimated to be at least 15 meters (49 feet) high. At the time, Maverick's was considered to be the biggest wave ever surfed. Two days later, a 10-meter (32 foot) wave dumped top professional rider Mark Foo and held him under until he died.

1 5

GLOSSARY

tubes – the barrel-like wave formations made by breaking waves as their crests arch over prior to collapsing

Maverick's is the biggest surf break in the United States. It lies on the Californian coast of the Pacific Ocean.

Xtreme Fact

The biggest day on record at Maverick's was October 28, 1999. Many top surfers refused to enter the water when wave faces peaked at around 18 meters (60 feet). The huge swell registered on seismographs in San Francisco, sparking fears that an earthquake had occurred.

An attempt to escape the crowds

When big wave surfing was gaining momentum, a major source of frustration remained for the world's most daring riders. They just could not paddle fast enough to ever stand a chance of dropping onto really big waves such as Jaws or some of the Waimea Bay monsters. That all changed in 1992, when a couple of surfers named Buzzy Kerbox and Laird Hamilton invented tow-in surfing.

Kerbox and Hamilton wanted to escape from Oahu's increasingly crowded, close-in waves. They wanted to surf at the offshore surfing grounds where massive waves break over the outer reefs rising steeply from the ocean floor. They made the trip out there in a Zodiac inflatable raft, using an outboard motor. Kerbox and Hamilton attached footstraps to their boards, and were towed behind the craft by a rope. They were able to ride big waves that no one else could get to.

KERBOX SUCCEEDS

In the winter of 1992, off the North Shore, Kerbox was towed into a wave approaching 15 meters in height. It wiped him out, and the wave behind it came tumbling down on him as well. Kerbox eventually found a way out. Then he went back to tackle the next monster. This time he succeeded.

THE JET SKI ADVANTAGE

Kerbox and Hamilton soon realized that a jet ski would give them an even greater speed advantage. It alone was capable of keeping up the same pace as the waves. The jet ski proved to be an excellent innovation. Now it became possible to catch waves of any size. Riding them without incident, however, was another matter.

Jet skis are used to tow surfers into giant waves too dangerous to paddle into.

Tow-in Surfing

The Hawaiian winter swells of 1997–98 produced the best surfing conditions in a century. Unfortunately, they also caused millions of dollars of damage and serious erosion of many beaches. The huge waves resulted from a weather phenomenon called El Niño.

The tow-in ride

It is difficult to imagine any surfing feat more exciting than to be towed into a North Shore giant. You come in fast and whip into position on the wave, with enough momentum to stay ahead of the breaking crest. As you skilfully carve a huge bottom turn upon the mountainous wall of water, the jet ski races away to wait for you at the end of the ride. After an all-too-brief 30 seconds of adrenalin-pumping excitement, you pull up onto the shoulder, in time for the jet ski pickup.

SHORTER, SPEEDIER BOARDS

Tow-in surfers use shorter, speedier boards than paddle-in surfers. You do not need the big board power once required to reach the crests of the waves. Footstraps hold you securely on the board during the tow.

Big Wednesday

On January 28, 1998, now remembered as 'Big Wednesday', the Pacific Ocean was whipped into a fury. The waves were so big that all of Oahu's North Shore beaches were declared officially off-limits to the public. Conditions became so severe that many professional riders refused to compete in the big wave contest to be held in honor of surfing legend Eddie Aikau. The waves were too big and too dangerous. Organizers cancelled the event.

BRADSHAW'S SPECIAL MOMENT

On Big Wednesday, 45-year old American surf veteran Ken Bradshaw desperately wanted to surf. When the competition was called off, Bradshaw and his partner, Dan Moore, went to nearby Outside Log Cabins, an outer reef. Moore towed Bradshaw into the biggest wave ever ridden on North Shore. It was estimated to be 25 meters (82 feet) in height. The historic moment was captured by IMAX cameras for the movie *Extreme*.

Hawaii's Mike Stewart demonstrates pipeline action on the bodyboard.

AN EXCITING ALTERNATIVE

A great new way to enjoy the surf was introduced on July 9, 1971, when Tom Morey invented the first bodyboard. The bodyboard offered an exciting alternative to the traditional surfboard. People could ride it in all wave conditions, from gently breaking, 2-meter (6.6 foot) beach waves, to huge arching barrels. Throughout the 1970s, bodyboarding continued to grow in popularity.

Mike Stewart's magic

It was in the early 1980s that the profile of the sport was given an enormous boost by a few gifted professional riders. The most prominent of these was Mike Stewart from Hawaii. Stewart's competitive career began in 1982. He quickly established himself as the world's most outstanding bodyboarder, and remained so for the next decade. Stewart constantly challenged himself to invent new maneuvers and set new limits for the sport. In big competitions, he never let the pressure get to him, even when the challenge from other competitors was tough. Stewart won a remarkable eight world bodyboarding titles in a career with many other successes.

Crispin Hughes bodyboards 'off the wall' in Hawaii, 1995.

Bodyboarding gear

Bodyboarders take to the surf in a wetsuit and swim fins. The fins are necessary for propelling the board onto the wave and through the water. The boards are shaped for maximum performance in all wave conditions. Riders wax their boards to provide the strong grip they need to remain on the board when performing tricks.

GLOSSARY

freefall – the action of falling from the crest of a wave to the trough below

plane – to ride flat upon the surface of the water

dropknee – a half-kneeling bodyboarding position

rail – the edge of the board

Xtreme Fact

Waimea Bay consistently has the largest waves on this planet. They require skill and a brave heart to ride. Hawaiian Phyllis Dameron, the first bodyboarder to surf these waves, would regularly **freefall** from the lips of 6-meter (20 foot) breakers.

Arm power and kick power

Bodyboarders use a combination of arm power and kick power to move through the water. The kick works best when the legs are held stiff and the fins are submerged. The arm power comes from stroking through the water, one arm at a time, as though swimming freestyle. Most board riders prefer to alternate between kick power and arm power to conserve energy.

Prone position

There are basically two ways to ride a bodyboard. In the prone position, you lie flat on the board and **plane** across the surface of the water. If both arms are not paddling, use one hand to hold the nose of the board steady. The board's speed increases when your legs are lifted clear of the water, freeing the board of drag.

Dropknee stance

In the **dropknee** stance favored by a number of riders, the bodyboarder assumes a half-kneeling position. There are a number of variations on this stance, but basically it involves propping up on your front foot and kneeling on your back leg. Most bodyboarders prefer frontside riding because they can face the wave and have a clear view of how it is breaking. In this stance, your right knee is able to apply pressure to the **rail** closest to the face of the wave.

Other bodyboarding greats

Two other bodyboarding greats are Michael Eppelstun and Brazilian Guilherme Tamega. Eppelstun, an Australian, was the first non-Hawaiian to win a world title. Like Stewart, he was an innovator. Among the new bodyboarding tricks introduced by Eppelstun are the backflip, the double el rollo and the air roll spin. The air roll spin, commonly known as the ARS, is regarded by many as the greatest bodyboarding maneuver. Tamega is now setting new standards in the sport. By the turn of the millennium he had won three world titles.

Find a good wave

Certain waves are well suited to bodyboarding. One of the best is a short, dumping **shorebreak**, where the waves form perfect tubes before exploding onto the sand. Wedging waves are created by swells reflecting off natural rock formations and side-washing into waves coming from another direction. The resulting clash doubles the wave power and creates a launching ramp for aerial stunts. Sucky reef waves occur when swells hit the reef and create steep take-offs. You can push into these waves early and freefall down the faces of the steepest sections.

Take off

Having paddled out beyond the surf line, watch the sets come in. When the right wave comes along, paddle into it, kicking hard as the wave pushes your board forward. Once you are on the face of the wave, stop paddling, slide back a little and angle the board in the direction you want to ride.

Match the wave speed

The main aim of angling the board across the wave face is to accelerate so your speed matches the speed of the wave. This helps you to make it across to the next section of the wave. Slide up and down the board until you find the best position for optimum speed.

Ride the tube

When you want to ride the tube formed by the arching wave, it often helps to stall, so that the curl begins to overtake you. Do this by dragging your legs through the water, putting pressure on the inside rail, or pulling up on the nose. The secret is to choose the exact time to release the stall.

When riding the tube, the secret is to choose the right time to release your stall.

Mike Stewart performing the bottom turn during a 1999 competition.

Xtreme Fact

A bodyboarder's landings are determined by the depth of the waves. Deep waves allow you to dive deep and penetrate to the back of the wave. Make sure you spread out when landing, to lessen your impact on shallower waves.

Learn to reverse spin and bottom turn

There are a number of basic maneuvers every bodyboarder must learn before tackling some of the sport's more advanced tricks. The reverse spin is a fairly simple, yet elegant, way to shift the board back towards the power source of the wave. Another essential part of bodyboarding is the bottom turn. Drop into the wave and accelerate down towards the trough, then switch direction at the bottom and head back into the wave. This propels you back into the wave face, well balanced and travelling at high speed. Many exciting moves can be launched from this position.

Stretch during freefall

When taking off from the crest of a steeply rearing, sucky wave, often you will be pitched into freefall ahead of the wave face. Learn to absorb the impact of landing in the trough from a significant height. The most effective method is to stretch the board well out in front of you during the freefall, and to try to land on the back corner of your board.

Try the backflip and air roll spin

The backflip is impressive. Leave the lip of the wave, then pull your board back sharply and flip your body and legs over in a complete rotation. The difficult part is landing flat so your board does not plough under the wave. The spectacular ARS combines a roll and a spin in one aerial maneuver. After projecting from the lip as high and far in front of the wave as possible, begin rolling, then midway through the roll, start spinning inward towards the face of the wave.

BOARDSAILING

Boardsailing, also known as 'sailboarding', combines the skills of sailing with the thrills of surfing.

THE WINDSURFER

During the 1960s, a Californian surfer named Hoyle Schweitzer came up with the idea of putting a sail on a surfboard. He got together with Jim Drake, an aeronautical engineer, who created an articulating sail rig, which allowed the sail to move about on the rig to catch the breeze. Between them, Schweitzer and Drake invented the sailboard. They formed a company to manufacture their new product, which they named the Windsurfer.

Windsurfing takes off

The original Windsurfer was quite clumsy in comparison with the sailboards of today. The board was heavy and very long. The sail rig was inefficient. It was, however, an innovation on traditional surfing, and thousands of enthusiasts took to the waves with their Windsurfers. The new sport took its name from the product, and became known as windsurfing. Clubs formed and races were organized. In the sport's early days, Robby Naish, a resident of Kailua Bay, Hawaii, was the undisputed champion.

A name change for the sport

As the sport grew, so did the need for more efficient, speedier equipment. New companies entered the market, causing the sport to be renamed boardsailing. This helped to avoid association with a single manufacturer's product.

improved design features

The introduction of several different harness types improved the sailboard design. The seat harness allowed riders to lean way out over the water, and to use this additional leverage for better control. Big surf still presented problems for boardsailors. In Hawaii, a couple of surfers came up with the idea of adding footstraps and sails to their boards. Before long, all sailboards came equipped with footstraps. Boardsailors began to ride the monster waves that pounded the reefs of Maui and Oahu, with some success.

SMALLER, LESS BUOYANT BOARDS

The boards riders use today are much smaller and less buoyant than the earlier ones. The lower **buoyancy** has resulted in boards that do not support your weight unless you are moving. This, of course, means that you cannot begin riding by standing up on the board. You need a water start.

Water start

For a water start, you lie alongside the board in the water, until the sail catches the wind. As the sailboard begins to move you are lifted onto the board. As the board accelerates, it becomes better suited to holding your weight. Soon, the board is planing on the surface of the water. A good board requires about seven knots of wind to begin planing.

Sailboard design variations

Today's sailboard designs vary to suit the different needs of boardsailors. Lighter boards provide better performance in high winds and big waves. Straighter boards with sharper rails, or edges, will reach higher speeds but are more difficult to turn. Rounder boards with smoother rails are great for stunts but do not move as fast. The recent development of short, wide boards with massive fins has made it possible to boardsail in the lightest wind conditions imaginable.

Different riding styles

Many people enjoy nothing better than to cruise on their sailboards. For those who prefer a bit more action, sailboard racing provides high speed drama, particularly if strong winds prevail. Slalom riders combine wily tactics with cracking pace and high velocity turns as they race each other from marker to marker. Freestyle riders push their boards to the limit, performing spectacular aerial flips, spins and other stunts that simply defy gravity.

Freestyle boardsailing allows riders to push their boards, and their skills, to the limits. Spectacular aerial stunts can be performed on the smaller, modern boards.

Xtreme Facts

An unusual variation of boardsailing was the introduction of gladiator races in 1998. The racing rules of the past 20 years were dispensed with, leading to a competition that now featured no protests, greater excitement and potential danger.

Wavesailing

Bold riding at Ho'okipa

Of all the forms of boardsailing, wavesailing is the most extreme. Wavesailing is an all-out assault on the biggest of waves. Ho'okipa, on the Hawaiian island of Maui, is considered to be the wavesailing capital of the world. Conditions there are just perfect for the sport. High winds and awesome waves are common. Bold riders accelerate into these mountainous waves as they thunder towards the shore. These incredible athletes often reach speeds in excess of 50 or 60 kilometers (31 to 37 miles) per hour as their boards skim straight up the towering wave faces and shoot several feet high above them into the air.

Wavesailors conquer Jaws

Maui is also home to the infamous Jaws, considered by many to be the biggest, baddest wave on Earth. Wavesailors were the first surf riders to tame Jaws. When they first succeeded in the 1980s, the breathtaking photos that resulted inspired a whole new generation of riders to take up the sport. The winter swells begin rolling in at around November each year, and the near-perfect tube formations of Hawaiian waves beckon wavesailors from all over the world. Ideal wave conditions for wavesailing are when open swells break parallel to the shore and strong winds are blowing along the beach.

Australian Phil McGain competing in the 1991 Aloha Classic, Hawaii.

Wakeboarding is the fastest-growing water sport in the world.

Xtreme Fact

A wakeboard boat requires much less power to pull a rider out of the water than a water skier. The larger surface area of the wakeboard ensures it will not dig into the water as a ski does. A wakeboarder planes at much lower speed than a skier does.

GLOSSARY

hybrid – any single thing composed of elements from different sources

take air – to be launched into the air from the crest of the wake or wave

phaser – a design feature at the bottom of a wakeboard that gives it a looser feel as it planes across the water's surface

The Hyperlite

The sport took a huge leap forward in 1990, when Herb O'Brien gathered together a group of top surfboard shapers from Hawaii. Their purpose was to create a new board design with better performance features. They came up with the slim Hyperlite, a board with neutral buoyancy, which made it much easier to submerge the board for starting in deep water. Other design improvements included the addition of a **phaser** on the bottom, which reduced the water's hold on the board and softened the landings from jumping the wake.

The wakeboarding boom

In recent times, the board has undergone further design changes. Many wakeboards now feature twin tails. Fins at both ends ensure the board will perform well regardless of the stance adopted by the rider. The result of these improvements was a board that was much easier to ride and capable of far more radical maneuvers than earlier ones had been. By the mid-1990s, the sport, now known as wakeboarding, had experienced a boom in popularity. Wakeboarding is the fastest-growing water sport in the world.

DESIGN DRAWBACKS

Footstraps were soon added to the Skurfer. Not only did they make it easier to stay on the board, but they also made it possible for riders to **take air** and carve bigger, snowboard-style turns. The Skurfer's biggest drawbacks were its narrow design and excessive buoyancy, which combined to make it quite difficult for many people to master. If a rider went for a spill, it was not easy to begin planing again from a deep water start. A number of enthusiasts persisted, however, and the sport of skiboarding was born.

Chrisophe Pouly performing a 180-degree air stunt on the wakeboard.

Wait in the water

Perhaps the easiest way to get up on a wakeboard is to wait in the water with your knees bent and the board parallel to the boat. As the boat accelerates, you will be lifted out of the water. Let the board turn as you plough through the water, and extend your legs when you feel pressure on them. Adopt a sideways stance, with your preferred foot forward.

Learn the basics

The ideal place to ride is where the wake forms the best shape. This is generally somewhere between 14 and 18 meters (46 and 60 feet) behind a boat travelling at an optimum speed of about 30 kilometers (19 miles) per hour. The wake should have good height, as it will form a launching pad for aerial stunts. Once up for the first time, find the right balance and learn to ride in a straight line. Turn by applying pressure to different parts of your board.

Cross the wakes

With the basic moves under control, learn to cross both wakes. Lean back slightly so that your board forms a carving edge. Turn your hips in the desired direction and, as the edge bites in, the board will begin to turn. Your knees must be bent to absorb the shock of the wake crossing. Turn your hips back the other way when your board has crossed to the other side. The board will race back across both wakes in the opposite direction. Multiple wake crossings at speed can be a lot of fun.

Wakeboarding Stunts

Take air

Taking air off the wake is exciting. Turn and accelerate towards the wake, holding the rope taut. It is important to dig in an edge with the board all the way to the wake, so it carves through the water. You must reach maximum speed at the crest of the wake. At this moment, extend your legs to provide extra spring from the wake into the air. Taking air is a special feeling, so try to hang there as long as possible before coming down to land. To do this, you must flatten out your board in the air, and you must try to stay balanced upon landing, because the rope will be slack for a moment.

Double up

For bigger air, nothing beats the double-up. This is when the boat driver makes a wide turn and then circles back into the oncoming wake. When the original wake meets the new wake, it doubles in size. This provides the perfect take-off ramp for some really big air tricks. A typical aerial stunt is the 180 air. To perform this stunt, launch off the wake facing forwards, then swing the tail of your board through half a circle to the front before you land backwards, or fakie.

Ride obstacles

Extreme stunt wakeboarders have taken the connection with skateboarding to new levels by placing ramps and fun boxes in the water. The boat brings you in close enough to slide along the rims of the obstacles before taking air from them. It is serious fun!

Xtreme Fact

Wakeboarding is a Summer X Games sport. In the freeride competition, riders complete two passes of at least five maneuvers and a double-up, where the really big stunts are performed. Judges look for intensity, style and execution.

Surf Jargon

amped
really fired up; enthusiastic

"Those breakers were big enough to get us really amped."

backdoor
to enter a tube from behind the peak of the wave

"I snuck in through the backdoor and still managed to shoot the tube."

closeout
what happens when a wave breaks across the whole beach simultaneously

"There were closeout conditions at Waimea Bay all week."

fakie
backwards

"She took air, did a 180 and landed fakie."

gnarly
awesome; really challenging

"The surf was gnarly for tow-in riders."

goofy
to ride with the right foot forward; as opposed to natural (left) foot stance

"He rides goofy."

green room
the space inside the tube

"I got the perfect ride through the green room."

grommet
an adolescent surfer

"She pulled some awesome moves for a grommet."

rinse cycle
the churning water that remains after a wave has broken

"He wiped out and was put through the rinse cycle."

slam the lip
to bounce off the top of a wave as it begins to curl

"I watched her slam the lip and pitch forward into freefall."

snake
to take someone else's wave; a violation of the unwritten surfers' code

"Don't ever try to snake my wave again."

vertical
a sharp upward movement on a wave

"She went vertical on a huge breaker."

Glossary

adrenaline rush
the special feeling that accompanies a thrilling experience

buoyancy
the ability to float on the surface of water

colossus
anything gigantic in size

dropknee
a half-kneeling bodyboarding position

freefall
the action of falling from the crest of a wave to the trough below

hybrid
any single thing composed of elements from different sources

hypothermia
a medical condition caused by the lowering of body temperature to dangerous levels

jet skis
small, motor-driven watercraft used for towing surfers into big waves and for performing fast rescues

neoprene
a synthetic rubber material used in the construction of wetsuits

phaser
a design feature on the bottom of a wakeboard that gives it a looser feel as it planes across the water's surface

plane
to ride flat upon the surface of the water

rail
the edge of the board

sets
series of waves

shorebreak
a wave that breaks upon the shore

swells
deep ocean waves

take air
to be launched into the air from the crest of the wake or wave

tow-in surfing
a form of surfing that requires the surfer to be towed onto big waves by jet ski

trough
the dip in the water surface at the foot of a breaking wave

tubes
the barrel-like wave formations made by breaking waves as their crests arch over prior to collapsing

wipeout
when a surfer is knocked from their board or tipped over by the force of the wave

Index